Mental Maths Tests

Key Stage 1

Other titles in this series:
Mental Maths Tests Key Stage 2
Mental Maths Tests Key Stage 3

Addison Wesley Longman Limited
Edinburgh Gate
Harlow, Essex CM20 2JE, England
and Associated Companies throughout the world

Published in the United States of America
by Addison Wesley Longman Publishing, New York

© Addison Wesley Longman Limited 1999

The rights of Brian Speed and Linda Terry to be identified as the authors of
this Work have been asserted by them in accordance with the Copyright,
Designs and Patents Act 1988.

All rights reserved; no part of this publication may be reproduced, stored in
a retrieval system, or transmitted in any form or by any means, electronic,
mechanical, photocopying, recording or otherwise without either the prior
written permission of the Publishers or a licence permitting restricted
copying in the United Kingdom issued by the Copyright Licensing Agency
Ltd, 90 Tottenham Court Road, London W1P 9HE.

First published 1999
ISBN 0 582 38189-4

British Library Cataloguing-in-Publication Data

A catalogue record for this book is available from the British Library.

Set by 36 in Stone Sans
Printed in Great Britain by Henry Ling Ltd., at the Dorset Press
Dorchester, Dorset

Contents

What this book covers **4**

    Mental Arithmetic at Key Stage 1 .... **4**

    Mathematics at Key Stage 1 .... **4**

    Levels of achievement **5**

    Using this book **6**

    Using the cassette **6**

    Helping your child improve **6**

Before you start **7**

Test 1 questions **8**

Pupil test sheet **10**

Test 2 questions **12**

Pupil test sheet **14**

Test 3 questions **16**

Pupil test sheet **18**

Answers and examiner's hints **20**

Checking your progress **32**

What this book covers

Mental Arithmetic at Key Stage 1

In recent years greater emphasis has been laid on the ability of children to solve mathematical questions in their heads, in other words, to do mental arithmetic. Since 1998 a Mental Arithmetic Paper has been part of the Mathematics Tests for pupils at Key Stage 2 (age 11) and Key Stage 3 (age 14). Although at present there is no Mental Arithmetic Paper at the end of Key Stage 1 (age 7), it is vital that your child begins to develop their ability in mental arithmetic as soon as possible. Indeed mental arithmetic is a key part of the 'National Numeracy Hour' to be introduced in all schools in 1999, and your child is likely to be faced with tests in mental arithmetic throughout their school career. Even in the *written* tests at Key Stage 1 (age 7) there are quite a few questions at the beginning of the paper which are spoken to the child by the teacher.

This book and cassette are designed to help your child develop their ability to solve mathematical questions and arithmetical problems in their head, i.e. to solve mental arithmetic problems.

It will help your child if they become familiar at Key Stage 1 with the type of mental arithmetic test that will actually be used at Key Stages 2 and 3. This involves a mental arithmetic test which is pre-recorded onto audio cassette and is played to the children. The test lasts about 20 minutes, with 20 questions to answer and a set time allowed for answering each question (here 10 seconds). The children write their answers in boxes on an answer sheet which has helpful information printed on it. The marks for this mental arithmetic test account for 20% of the total marks given for mathematics at later Key Stages, so it is important in determining the *level* that your child will achieve.

Mathematics at Key Stage 1

During the first two years at school your child will cover Key Stage 1 of the National Curriculum. Towards the end of Year 2 (at age 7) he or she will take the National Curriculum Tests in Mathematics and English (often referred to as SATs – Standard Assessment Tasks). These written tests are taken in your child's own school and are carried out under the supervision of their own teachers. They are marked within the school, but external moderators will then check the marks to make sure that the same standards have been applied in all schools.

The National Curriculum divides Mathematics at Key Stage 1 into three sections called Attainment Targets (ATs)

AT1 Using and Applying Mathematics

AT2 Number

AT3 Shape, Space and Measures

AT1, Using and Applying Mathematics, is assessed by your child's teacher in the classroom. It is the other two ATs (AT2 and AT3) that are assessed in the National Tests. Children working at *Level 1* in Mathematics will usually undertake practical mathematical tasks under the supervision of their teacher. Children who are assessed by their teacher to be working *beyond Level 1* will take a written test, usually in May of Year 2.

The results of the written National Tests for KS1 Mathematics will be available to you, as parents, by the end of July of Year 2 (age 7). Your child's results will be expressed as a level for each subject assessed. As well as the level for the written tests in Mathematics, you will also receive the results of the classroom assessments made by your child's teacher of work undertaken during the year (called 'Teacher Assessment').

You will also receive a summary of the Key Stage 1 results in Mathematics achieved by all the other students in your school, and for all students nationally. You will then be able to check your child's progress against other students of the same age.

Levels of achievement

At Key Stage 1, each subject is divided into Levels 1 to 3. By the end of Year 2 (age 7), most children should be working at Levels 1 to 3, although in some cases children may still be said to be 'working towards' Level 1.

On average, most children will achieve Level 2 by the end of Year 2 (age 7) and a few will reach Level 3. Only very rarely will a child achieve Level 4.

The table on the right illustrates the percentages of students nationally who are expected to gain each level. Clearly most children achieve one of the 'bands' in Level 2.

Percentage of students reaching a particular Level in Mathematics at Key Stage 1

Level	Percentage
1	15
2C *at the threshold of Level 2*	20
2B *in the middle of Level 2*	25
2A *towards the top of Level 2*	30
3	10

Using this book

This book and the accompanying cassette, concentrates on Mental Arithmetic and is appropriate for students aged 7 at the end of Key Stage 1. Each of the three sections contains a complete Mental Arithmetic Test for practice, of the type your child will face at Key Stages 2 and 3.

Before you start gives the information you will need about the tests. The **Test questions** are printed so that you can see what is on the tape. Then there are **Pupil test sheets** for your child to complete while listening to the tape and towards the end of the book you will find the **answers** to each test, including helpful tips to improve your child's understanding of mental arithmetic. At the end of the book **Checking your progress** provides a **marking grid** to indicate the *level* your child has reached in each test.

Using the cassette

You will find clear instructions on the cassette about how to proceed and some instructions before each of the Test questions.

Helping your child improve

After your child has completed a test, and you have checked the answers and identified the level achieved, it is important to look for any possible areas of improvement.

These suggestions may help to improve your child's score:

- Identify any questions that have not been attempted or in which an error has been made.
- Talk about the reason why that question was missed or a mistake was made
  – was it due to a misunderstanding of the question?
  – was it due to an error in calculation?
  – was it due to lack of time to think about the problem?
- Look at the question together (on the pages for the Test questions). Pick out the key words or ideas in that question so that your child can more readily identify what is required.
- Let your child try the question again and check whether they can get the correct answer once the question has been understood. Examiner hints alongside many answers might help if your child still has difficulty finding the right answer.
- If the reason for an error seems to be a lack of time, then your child can try the other timed tests in this book and cassette. Practice really does help a child get used to working in the time available.

Before you start

You will need;
- a cassette player,
- a cassette containing the tests,
- a pencil or pen,
- the **pupil test sheet**

then
- listen to the first part of the test which gives you instructions. Stop when you hear a bleep.
- make sure that you understand what you will have to do.

There are 20 questions in each test, and each question will be said **twice**. There will be a 10 second pause for your child to answer each question, but if they need longer, stop the tape until they have had time to think it through and write down an answer. Then start the tape again. There is a **Pupil Test Sheet** with boxes for each question in which to write the answer, and some questions have information printed in the box or by the side of the box. **Make sure that your child understands that this information will be useful when answering that question.** If your child can't answer a question, tell them to draw a cross in that box, or if they want to change an answer, tell them to draw a cross through the incorrect answer and write the correct one next to it. Encourage your child to work out the answers in their head.

Note to Parents

Start the tape and listen carefully with your child to the *instructions*.

Stop the tape when you hear a bleep and check that your child understood what to do.

- Start the tape again and let your child answer the **practice question**.
- Stop the tape when instructed and check that the answer to the practice question has been written in the correct box.
- Start the tape again and let your child work through the test.
- Stop the tape at the end of the test (about 20 minutes).
- The test questions are in this book to help you see what is on the tape.
- Check your child's answers with the **answers and examiner's hints** (page 20); giving 1 mark for each correct answer.
- Count the marks and identify the level your child has achieved using the **marking grid** in **Checking your progress** (page 32).
- Follow through the suggested ways to help your child improve (page 6).

Test 1 questions

These are the questions recorded on the tape. Each question is read out **twice** and has a 10 second pause before going on to the next question.

Practice question   Add together six and five

 You are now going to begin the test.

1   Add together nine and seven.

2   Look at the numbers in the box numbered two.
     Draw a ring around any even numbers.

3   Emily has ten pence. She spends six pence.
     How much does she have now?

4   Look at the shapes in the box numbered four.
     Put a tick in the rectangle.

5   Three apples are each cut in half.
     How many halves are there?

6   Subtract nine from fifteen.

7   Look at the numbers in the box numbered seven.
     What do you think the next number should be?

8   Multiply five by five.

9   Look at the numbers in the box numbered nine.
     Draw a ring around the largest number.

10   A chocolate bar weighs fifty grams. Joshua eats half of it.
     How much chocolate is left?

Test 1 questions

11 Look at the sums in the box numbered eleven.
Draw a ring around the sum whose answer is nine.

12 Joseph saves twenty pence each week.
How much will he save in two weeks?

13 Mrs Pace has three pots with four pencils in each pot.
How many pencils does she have altogether?

14 Look at the shapes in the box numbered fourteen.
Draw a tick in the pentagon.

15 Look at the sum in the box numbered fifteen.
Which sign will make the sum correct?

16 Sheena buys a pen which costs forty nine pence.
She has one pound. How much change will she be given?

17 Look at the clocks in the box numbered seventeen.
They show when playtime starts and finishes.
How long does playtime last?

18 A ribbon is forty centimetres long.
Mrs Smith cuts it exactly in half. How long is each piece?

19 Add together eighteen and one hundred.

20 Look at the coins in the purse in the box numbered twenty.
How much money is there?

Go to page 20 for the answers.
On the Pupil test sheet give 1 mark for each correct answer.

Pupil test sheet — Test 1

Practice question

[ ]

1. [ ]
2. 7   10   13   15   18
3. [   ]   p | 10p   6p
4. △ ▭ ⬠ ⬡ ▱
5. [   ]   🍎 🍎 🍎
6. [   ]   9   15
7. 30,   25,   20,   15,   ……
8. [   ]
9. 119   59   209   29
10. [   ] grams | 50 grams
11. 12−4   14−5   16−6

Marks: 1, 2, 3, 4, 5, 6, 7, 8, 9, 10, 11

Pupil test sheet Test

Marks

| 12 | | p | 20p | | 12 |
| 13 | | pencils | | | 13 |

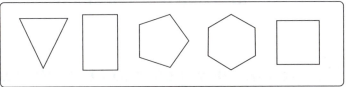

14					14
15			6 ? 2 = 3		15
16		p	49p £1		16
17		minutes	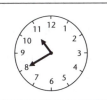		17
18		cm	40 cm		18
19					19
20		p			20

Test 2 questions

These are the questions recorded on the tape. Each question is read out **twice** and has a 10 second pause before going on to the next question.

Practice question   Add together ten and five

 You are now going to begin the test.

1   Add together two and five.

2   Look at the numbers in the box numbered two.
    Draw a ring round the number forty five.

3   What is the next odd number after nineteen?

4   Look at the shapes in the box numbered four.
    Put a tick in the triangle.

5   What is eight take away three?

6   Look at the clock in the box numbered six.
    Write down the time it shows.

7   What number is five more than thirty?

8   How many quarters are there in one whole one?

9   Look at the numbers in the box numbered nine.
    Draw a ring around the smallest number.

10 What is half of sixteen?

11 What is ten times four?

Test 2 questions

12 Write down any even number which is larger than ten and smaller than twenty.

13 How many sides has a hexagon?

14 It started raining at four o'clock. It rained for three hours.
In the box numbered fourteen, tick the clock which shows the time when it stopped raining.

15 I share twenty pence equally between four children.
How much does each child receive?

16 Simon had twenty conkers. He gave seven conkers to Hecham.
How many conkers has Simon now?

17 Look at the number line in the box numbered seventeen.
What number does the arrow point to?

18 What is twenty two add forty five?

19 Look at the sum in the box numbered nineteen.
What number will make this sum correct?

20 Joy has ten sweets. She shares them equally with Anna.
How many do they each have?

Go to page 24 for the answers.

On the Pupil test sheet give 1 mark for each correct answer.

Pupil test sheet   Test

Practice question

Marks

1

2   37   45   56   79

3

4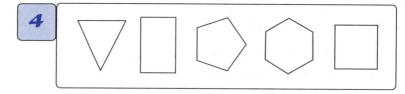

5

6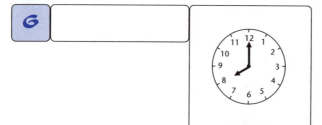

7

8

9   65   42   39   18   20

Pupil test sheet   Test 2

Marks

10

11

12

13 hexagon

14
4 o'clock

15 p   20p

16 conkers   20 conkers

17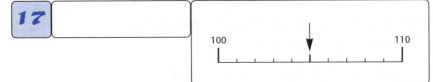
100   110

18   22   45

19   ? – 15 = 6

20

Test 3 questions

These are the questions recorded on the tape. Each question is read out **twice** and has a 10 second pause before going on to the next question.

Practice question   Take away six from ten

 You are now going to begin the test.

1   Subtract six from fourteen.

2   Look at the numbers in the box numbered two. Draw a ring around any number that can be divided by three exactly.

3   Add together eleven and five.

4   Multiply six by ten.

5   Look at the number line in the box numbered five. What number does the arrow point to?

6   Look at the line drawn in the box numbered six. How long do you think it is?

7   Jack faces North. He makes a quarter turn. Which way might he now be facing?

8   What is half of eight?

9   Mary leaves home at eight o'clock. It takes her thirty minutes to walk to school. At what time does she arrive there?

10   Ali has four ten pence coins. How much does she have?

Test 3 questions

11 Look at the shapes in the box numbered eleven. Put a tick in any shapes that have right angles.

12 Rosie buys a carton of drink costing twenty pence and a bar of chocolate costing seventeen pence.
How much does she spend?

13 Write the number seventy six in figures.

14 Look at the sum in the box numbered fourteen.
What number will make it correct?

15 Look at the coins in the box numbered fifteen.
How much money is there?

16 What is the difference between nine and fifteen?

17 How many sides has a pentagon?

18 Look at the numbers in the box numbered eighteen.
What do you think the missing number should be?

19 What is the sum of three, five and four?

20 George and Harry share one pound equally.
How much do they each have?

Go to page 28 for the answers.

On the Pupil test sheet give 1 mark for each correct answer.

Pupil test sheet Test 3

Practice question

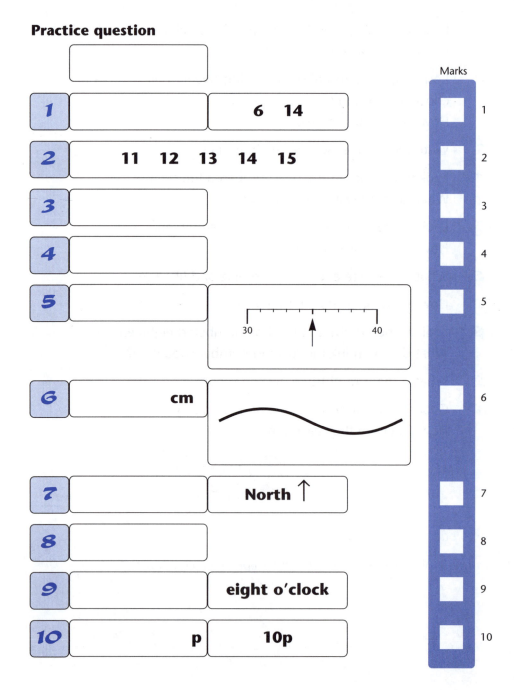

Pupil test sheet — Test 3

11

12 _____ p   20p   17p

13 _____

14 _____   ? + 9 = 26

15 _____ pence

16 _____   9   15

17 _____   pentagon

18 _____   101   102   ?   104   105

19 _____   3   5   4

20 _____

Answers and examiner's hints Test 1

Practice question   11

1   **16**

Hint Plenty of practice in addition and subtraction will improve the speed and accuracy of your child's mental arithmetic. Sometimes it helps to make use of 10's, so 9 + 7 is the same as 10 + 6, adding 1 to make the 9 a 10 and subtracting 1 to make the 7 a 6.

2   **10** and **18**

Hint Make sure your child understands that *even* numbers are all those that can be divided exactly by two. They all end in one of the digits 0, 2, 4, 6 or 8. All numbers that cannot be divided exactly by two are *odd* numbers.

3   **4p**

Hint Identify the key words in this type of question so that your child can quickly recognise the type of problem involved. Here the key words are 'has', 'spends' and 'have now' This is a *subtraction* problem, with 10 pence minus 6 pence equals 4 pence.

4   **The tick should be in the second shape**

Hint Look at objects in the home and identify them as squares, triangles, rectangles, circles, etc. In a *rectangle*, the opposite sides have the same length and are parallel. (This is different from the *square* which has all its sides the same length and parallel.)

5   **6**

Hint: Imagine three apples cut into halves, you should see six pieces. You might even cut three similar objects into halves to give your child a visual demonstration of this idea.

Answers and examiner's hints — Test 1

6 **6**

Hint Encourage good mental arithmetic here by again making use of 10s. Here subtract 10 from 15 to get 5, then add 1 on to get 6.

7 **10**

Hint Predicting the next number in a sequence is a useful skill. Notice how the numbers get five smaller each time, so the next number is just five less than fifteen, which is ten.

8 **25**

Hint Practice with tables is the best way to learn them. Check your child knows their 5 times table.

9 **209**

Hint Look for the number(s) with the most digits, then identify the number with the largest first digit.

10 **25 grams**

Hint Although this question involves *halving*, it will also be helpful to be familiar with *doubling*. Your child will then recognise that doubling 25 grams will give 50 grams.

11 **14 – 5**

Hint This is best done by recognising that $12 - 4 = 8$, and $16 - 6 = 10$, so the other one must be the correct one. Check this by again using the idea of 10's, with $10 - 5$, add 4 gives the answer 9. Remind your child that the word 'sums' in the question can mean add, subtract, multiply or divide. Here the word refers to subtract.

Answers and examiner's hints — Test 1

12 40p

Hint Look for the key words , 'each week' and 'two weeks'. The answer involves multiplying 20p by 2 to give 40p.

13 12

Hint Look for the key words , 'in each pot' , 'altogether'. The answer involves multiplying 4 pencils by 3 to give 12 pencils.

14 The tick should be in the third shape

Hint Check that your child is confident in identifying squares, rectangles, triangles, etc. Children often confuse pentagon (5 sided) and hexagon (6 sided).

15 Divide ($\div$)

Hint Remind your child that the key word 'sum' can mean add, subtract, multiply or divide. Look at the answer, it is smaller than the six, so it must be either subtraction or division. Try each one and your child will see that it has to be 'divide', since $6 \div 2 = 3$ but $6 - 2 = 4$.

16 51p

Hint Look for the key words, 'buys', 'costs 49p', 'has £1', 'change'. Your child will also need to know that there are 100 pence in £1. This is a *subtraction* problem with 100p – 49p = 51p. Again you could make use of 10's, in this case multiples of 10's, since $100 - 50 = 50$, then add an extra 1 to give 51 (since only 49 is subtracted).

Answers and examiner's hints   *Test* **1**

17   **15 minutes**

Hint Show your child that on this type of clock the big hand takes five minutes to move between each number. Since the big hand has moved on by 3 numbers (from 5 to 8), then 5 minutes $\times$ 3 equals 15 minutes.

18   **20 cm**

Hint Encourage good mental arithmetic by *halving* the 4 to give 2 and so making half of 40 into 20. Again we are making use of the idea of 10's, this time seeing 40 and 20 as multiples of 10's, by 4 and 2 respectively. You can also encourage your child to check their answer by *doubling* it, to give the original amount ($2 \times 20 = 40$).

19   **118**

Hint This type of question is easily practised, and then remembered. However you can again make use of 10's by adding 20 to 100, giving 120, then taking away 2 to leave 118.

20   **32p**

Hint Add the tens (or multiples of ten) first, then the pennies on to this. So we have $3 \times 10 = 30$, then add 2 to give 32.

Answers and examiner's hints — Test 2

Practice question   15

1   7

Hint This type of question should give a good confidant start. You can use 7 objects and place them into one group of 5 and one group of 2, before getting your child to count them if they have trouble with this question.

2   45

Hint Your child should recognise the first digit as the tens, so look for the number with the four first. The second digit is the units, so the 5 should appear here.

3   21

Hint Remember that the odd numbers go up in two's, so just add two on to nineteen to give 21. You could ask your child to list all the odd numbers from 1 to, say, 31 for practice.

4   The tick should be in the first shape

Hint Look for triangles around the home, they need to be recognised. Triangles have three sides. On car journeys you could look for different shapes on road signs, some of which use triangles.

5   5

Hint There are a few different words for subtract, such as take away, difference between; so try to be familiar with each one.

Answers and examiner's hints — Test 2

6 8 o'clock

Hint Practise reading the time using clocks around the home. Help your child be aware of the hour 'hand' of the clock and the minute 'hand' (which is larger).

7 35

Hint Start from the thirty, and count on five. Practise this type of addition. Look carefully at the words 'more than' which suggest adding.

8 4

Hint Check your child understands that a quarter is a whole divided into four equal parts. Your could ask extra questions about one third, one half, etc.

9 18

Hint Since they are all tens and units, look for the smallest tens, that is the smallest first number, which is 1. So the smallest is 18. Ideas of *smallest* and *largest* are often tested. You could ask your child to identify the largest number in the box!

10 8

Hint Think of what is *doubled* to get sixteen. Use other examples to help your child to see that the ideas of halving and doubling are closely related. You can check the answer to a halving question by doubling it; and vice versa.

Answers and examiner's hints — Test 2

11 40

Hint The ten times table is an important one to learn. Check that your child knows it.

12 any of 12 or 14 or 16 or 18

Hint The key words are 'even numbers', 'larger than 10', and 'smaller than 20'. The even numbers need to be identified, with two dividing exactly into them.

13 6

Hint Children do get mixed up with hexagon (6 sides) and pentagon (5 sides). It may help your child to remember that the sound of hex is almost like six, so six sides to the hexagon.

14 tick the third clock showing 7 o'clock

Hint Practise counting on in hours with your child using a clock face. Then try it without the clock face.

15 5p

Hint 'Share and 'divide' are the same. So the question is really 20p divided by 4, which gives 5p.

16 13 conkers

Hint The key is to recognise this is a *subtraction* problem. So 20 take away 7, gives 13.

Answers and examiner's hints Test ②

17 105

> **Hint** Your child needs to recognise that they are looking for the number *halfway* between 100 and 110. Looking for halfway between 0 and 10 , gives 5, then add this to the 100, giving 105.

18 67

> **Hint** Add the *units* in your head, 2 + 5 = 7, then add the *tens* in your head 20 + 40 = 60, which should lead to 60 + 7 = 67.

19 21

> **Hint** Remember that 'sum' can mean add, subtract, multiply or divide. Here the sum shown in the box involves subtract. However the answer must be a number which is six *bigger than* the 15. So add six on to the 15, to give 21.

20 5

> **Hint** The key words are 'shares them equally', which will suggest 'divides'. Since there are 2 people, we have 10 ÷ 2 = 5.

Answers and examiner's hints — Test 3

Practice question   4

1   8

   Hint First, take four from fourteen, giving you ten, then take two from the ten to give you eight.

2   12 or 15

   Hint Look for any number in the three times table. The numbers 12 (4 × 3) and 15 (5 × 3) appear in the three times table and can therefore be divided by 3 exactly.

3   16

   Hint Add the units first, which is five add one, then add the ten.

4   60

   Hint The ten times table should be learnt off-by-heart.

5   35

   Hint Look halfway between thirty and forty, which is thirty five. You could check that your child is aware that halfway between 0 and 10 is 5, then add 30 to give 35.

6   Accept any answer between 4 cm and 7 cm

   Hint the line should be estimated in centimetres. You might encourage an estimate based on the fact that their fingers are about 1 cm wide.

Answers and examiner's hints — Test 3

7 — East or West

Hint The points of the compass can be learnt by a little phrase such as "Never Eat Slimy Worms". The key words are 'faces North' and 'quarter turn'.

8 — 4

Hint It might help to imagine eight pence divided into two piles of four pence. The word 'of' suggests multiply, so $\frac{1}{2} \times 8 = 4$.

9 — 8.30

Hint Imagine a clock face showing half an hour after eight o'clock. Encourage your child to recognise that thirty minutes is half an hour. Use an actual clock to demonstrate this if you can. The ideas of a.m. and p.m. do not matter here.

10 — 40p

Hint This needs recognising as simply four times ten. Encourage your child to practise the 10 times table.

11 — The **square** and **rectangle** should both be ticked, i.e. shapes one and four

Hint Recognise the right angles as the corners of windows or doors.

Answers and examiner's hints Test 3

12 **37p**

Hint Add the units first to give 7p, then the tens to give 30p, put them both together to get 37 pence.

13 **76**

Hint Write it as you hear it, seventy first, then the six. Remember the tens are the first digit (number) and the units the second digit.

14 **17**

Hint Remember 'sum' can mean add, subtract, multiply or divide. Here the box shows add. The number we need must add on to 9 to give 26 as the answer. We therefore need to *count up* from the 9, so we go one up to 10, then ten up to 20, then six up to 26, this gives is 1 + 10 + 6 = 17 altogether.

15 **66p**

Hint Add the coins which are multiples of tens, to get 60p, then add the pennies to get 6p, then add them both together to get 66p

16 **6**

Hint Remember that 'difference' is another word for *subtraction*, so take 9 away from 15, by taking away ten and then adding one back. So 15 − 10 = 5, then add one to give 6.

Answers and examiner's hints Test ③

17 5

> *Hint* There is often confusion between the pentagon (5 sides) and the hexagon (6 sides). You could look at the third shape in the box numbered 11 (the pentagon) and compare it with the second shape (the hexagon).

18 103

> *Hint* Don't be confused by the size of the numbers, just look at the beginning two digits because they are all 10… The pattern should then be easy to spot. It goes up by one each time. So 103 is the missing number.

19 12

> *Hint* "What is the sum of" means add them together. Here 'sum' is *not* used to mean an operation involving add, subtract, multiply or divide. The extra word, 'of', after 'sum' is important here.

20 50p

> *Hint* As long as the fact that £1 = 100 pence is remembered, then the problem is straightforward. The key words are 'share equally' and, since there are two people, we are *dividing* by two. So 100 pence ÷ 2 = 50 pence.

Checking your progress

Now complete the marking grid for your child's attempt at each test, then use the **Guide to level achieved**.

Marking grid

	Correct	
Test 1		out of 20
Test 2		out of 20
Test 3		out of 20

Guide to level achieved

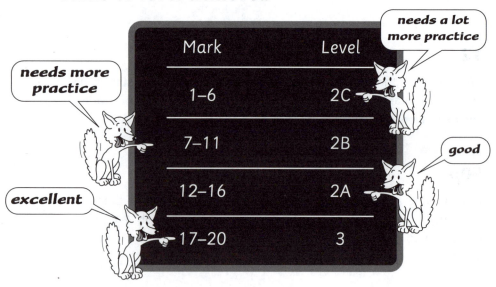

Mark	Level
1–6	2C
7–11	2B
12–16	2A
17–20	3

needs a lot more practice — 2C
needs more practice — 2B
good — 2A
excellent — 17–20

No Level 1 is awarded in this Mental Arithmetic Test, whatever the score. For advice on improving the score turn to **Helping your child improve** on page 6.